The Amazing Ground

Cookbook

Quick and Easy Ground Beef Recipes to Delight Your Family

BY - Charlotte Long

♡♡♡ ♡♡ ♡♡ ♡♡ ♡ ♡♡ ♡♡ ♡♡ ♡♡♡

License Page

No part of this book and its content should be transmitted in any format for commercial and personal use without asking for permission from the author in writing.

The purpose of the content is to enlighten you and pass cooking knowledge to you in a straightforward way. Hence, the author is not responsible for any implications and assumptions drawn from the book and its content.

Table of Contents

Introduction

Ground beef is equivalent to countless possibilities. As long as you know how to cook the meat right. Almost every ground beef recipe starts with proper browning to let the flavors ooze out and create a nice crust that's delicious to the bite. But of course, picking the freshest meat from the market can make or break the outcome of your recipe. So, make sure you get the package with the farthest sell-by date. If you are not cooking it immediately, store the package in the freezer until you are ready to add it to one of the recipes in our collection. Speaking of our recipe collection, take a sneak peek of what's delicious to come for you in this cookbook through this list:

- Korean Ground Beef and Rice Bowl

- Italian Meatballs
- Thai Basil Beef
- Mexican Black Bean Chili
- Moroccan Meatball Soup
- Japanese Ginger Ground Beef
- Swedish Meatballs
- Mongolian Ground Beef
- Chinese Beef Dumplings
- Beef Shakshuka
- Stuffed Cabbage
- Stuffed Peppers
- Beef Rolls
- Classic Meatloaf
- Grilled Beef and Cheese
- Meatballs Sub Sandwich
- Juicy Hamburger
- Lasagna Soup
- Taco Soup
- Hamburger Stroganoff
- Shepherd's Pie
- Ground Beef and Broccoli Stir-Fry
- Creamy Ground Beef and Shells
- Ground Beef Pasta Skillet
- Classic Spaghetti
- Beef Lasagna
- Ground Beef Nachos
- Ground Beef and Cabbage Salad

- Spicy Ground Beef & Cucumber Salad
- Lettuce Wraps

Ready to grind in the kitchen with ground beef? Let's start cooking delicious meals for you and your family!

1. Korean Ground Beef and Rice Bowl

One of the various meals where ground beef could make magic is in rice bowls. This Korean-inspired dish is easy to make and even easier to love because you can tailor it according to your taste. You can adjust the ingredients to suit your palate and make use of whatever is in your pantry. You can serve it with as many vegetables to make it healthier or as little if you are not too fond of the fresh veggie taste. It really is up to you.

Serving Size: 4

Prep Time: 25 mins

Ingredients:

- 1 lb. lean ground beef
- 4 cups cooked rice
- 6 pcs green onions, chopped and divided
- 1 tbsp fresh ginger, grated
- 5 garlic cloves, crushed
- 2 tsp toasted sesame oil
- 1/2 cup soy sauce
- 1 tbsp toasted sesame seeds
- 1/4 tsp red pepper flakes, crushed
- 1/3 cup brown sugar

Instructions:

Heat skillet on medium-high fire and add beef to brown, stirring and breaking apart into small pieces, for about five minutes.

Add ginger, garlic, and sesame oil and stir for another two minutes.

Pour in soy sauce and sprinkle sugar and crushed red pepper flakes. Continue to cook for another seven minutes, stirring occasionally.

Add half of the chopped green onions, stir, and turn off the fire.

Divide hot cooked rice among individual bowls, spoon ground beef mixture on top, then sprinkle with the remaining green onions, plus sesame seeds.

Serve and enjoy.

2. Italian Meatballs

Meatballs and ground beef are almost always in the same sentence. It is one recipe that can be made in many ways and still come out delightful. For our first ground beef recipe (that means you can expect more later), we are making an Italian-style dish highlighted with a rich tomato sauce, Parmesan, olive oil, and spices. Need we say more?

Serving Size: 5

Prep Time: 35 mins

Ingredients:

- 1 and 1/2 lbs. ground beef
- 1/4 cup Parmesan cheese, freshly grated
- 3/4 cup breadcrumbs
- 1/2 cup parsley, finely chopped
- 1-15oz can crushed tomatoes
- 1/2 cup onion, finely chopped
- 2 tbsp garlic, minced and divided
- 4 pcs bay leaves
- 1/4 cup tomato paste
- 1/4 cup milk
- 1 pc egg
- 2 tbsp olive oil
- 1 tsp Italian seasoning
- 1 and 1/2 tsp salt, divided
- 1 tsp ground black pepper, divided

Instructions:

Stir together beef, breadcrumbs, Parmesan, one tablespoon of minced garlic, parsley, milk, egg, Italian seasoning, and about one teaspoon of salt and half a teaspoon of freshly ground black pepper until well blended.

Form beef mixture into meatballs of your desired size. Make sure to keep them uniform to cook them evenly.

Heat olive oil in a skillet over medium-high and slowly add meatballs to brown, often stirring, for about eight minutes. Remove from the pan with a slotted spoon and set aside.

Using the same skillet, sauté the remaining garlic and onion for a minute.

Add tomatoes with their juices, tomato paste, and bay leaves. Sprinkle with the remaining salt and pepper. Adjust to taste.

Put the meatballs back into the skillet and let it simmer for a few minutes until the meat is cooked through. Serve and enjoy.

3. Thai Basil Beef

Do Thai basil and ground beef sound like a simple meal idea? You bet! This savory and a bit spicy dish will hit big the first time for its simplicity but undeniably tasty makeup. It does not require too many ingredients but may need you to prepare a lot of hot steamed rice to pair it up. With every spoonful, you wouldn't resist its rich taste that explodes in the mouth.

Serving Size: 4

Prep Time: 25 mins

Ingredients:

- 1 lb. lean ground beef
- 1 pc bell pepper, seeded and thinly sliced
- 1 pc sweet onion, thinly sliced
- 6 cloves garlic, minced
- 1 cup fresh basil leaves, divided
- 1 tbsp fresh cilantro, chopped finely
- 2 tbsp olive oil
- 1 tbsp brown sugar
- 2 tbsp fresh lime juice
- 1 tbsp chili paste
- 2 tbsp soy sauce
- 1 tbsp fish sauce

Instructions:

Whisk together lime juice, chili paste, soy sauce and fish sauce, plus brown sugar in a small bowl until the sugar is dissolved. Set aside.

Meanwhile, heat oil in a skillet on medium-high fire and add beef to brown for about six minutes, stirring and breaking apart to create an even crust.

Stir in bell peppers, onions, and garlic and continue to cook for another five minutes, stirring occasionally.

Gently pour prepared sauce mixture, plus basil leaves. Let it sizzle for a few minutes until the basil leaves are wilted.

Garnish with freshly chopped cilantro and serve.

4. Mexican Black Bean Chili

Chili is another delightful way to enjoy ground beef. This Mexican recipe will never disappoint with its chunky and tasty character. It has the right blend of spices and a decent mix of meat and veggies for the ultimate feast. If you are looking for a quick and easy meal you can serve for lunch or dinner with rice or rolls, this is what you need to make your busy weeknights delightful, still, for everyone.

Serving Size: 6

Prep Time: 20 mins

Ingredients:

- 1 lb. ground beef
- 1 cup green bell pepper, seeded and diced
- 1 cup onion, diced
- 3 cloves garlic, crushed
- 6 tbsp fresh cilantro, finely chopped
- 2-15oz cans black beans, rinsed and drained
- 2-14.5oz cans diced tomatoes
- 6 tbsp sour cream
- 1 and 1/2 cups beef broth
- 1 and 1/2 tsp ground cumin
- 3/4 tsp dried oregano
- 1 tbsp chili powder
- 1/2 tsp salt
- 1/8 tsp ground black pepper

Instructions:

Heat a skillet on medium-high fire and add beef to brown, stirring and breaking apart the meat with the back of the spoon.

Drain grease and put back the beef into the skillet together with the onions and bell peppers. Stir for another minute or two until the veggies are crisp-tender.

Add garlic and stir for another minute.

Sprinkle with cumin, oregano, chili powder, salt, and pepper.

Add tomatoes with all its juices, plus beans and broth.

Let the mixture simmer for 15 minutes on low heat with a lid, until it becomes slightly thick. Stir occasionally to keep the bottom from sticking.

To serve, ladle chili into individual bowls, dot with sour cream, and garnish with freshly chopped cilantro.

5. Moroccan Meatball Soup

Now, here is another dish from a foreign cuisine that makes use of ground beef smartly. It's a soup dish from Morocco, complete with spices and herbs that make it authentic. If the aroma of this dish is a standout with harissa and cumin, imagine how delicious it tastes once you have a spoonful.

Serving Size: 4

Prep Time: 40 mins

Ingredients:

- 1 lb. lean ground beef
- 1/2 cup whole-wheat couscous
- 4 pcs carrots, sliced into 1-inch pieces
- 4 cups baby spinach
- 1 and 1/2 cups fresh cilantro, roughly chopped and divided
- 1 cup scallions, roughly chopped
- 1 tbsp extra-virgin olive oil
- 1 pc egg, lightly beaten
- 4 cups chicken broth
- 2 cups water
- 2 tbsp harissa, divided
- 1 and 1/2 tsp ground cumin, divided
- 1 tsp Kosher salt

Instructions:

Place one cup of cilantro and scallions in a food processor and pulse to a coarse puree.

Place half of the cilantro mixture in a large bowl and add beef, one tablespoon of harissa, and egg. Sprinkle with half a teaspoon each of cumin and salt and mix to blend. Form mixture into balls and set aside.

Heat oil in a pot over medium fire and sauté carrots for five minutes or until they start to brown.

Add the remaining half of the cilantro-scallions mixture, plus the remaining tablespoon of harissa and another half a teaspoon each of cumin and salt.

Pour chicken broth and water, then boil.

Gently add the meatballs and cook in a simmer on low heat for eight minutes, stirring occasionally.

Finally, add couscous and spinach and let it cook for another five minutes, or until the couscous becomes tender. Adjust the seasoning as needed.

To serve, ladle soup in bowls and garnish with the remaining cilantro and a pinch of cumin.

6. Japanese Ginger Ground Beef

Soboro Donburi is one of the best-tasting recipes Japan has made out of ground beef. It's a rice bowl highlighted by ginger-flavored ground beef with some peas for a bite and keep the dish balanced. This dish only requires five ingredients and a hot skillet to get you digging into a delectable and filling bowl.

Serving Size: 4

Prep Time: 30 mins

Ingredients:

- 1 lb. ground beef
- 2 cups steamed hot rice
- 1 cup frozen peas
- 1 tbsp ginger, minced
- 1/3 cup soy sauce
- 1/4 cup water
- 1 tbsp sugar

Instructions:

Place meat, soy sauce, and water in a skillet. Sprinkle with sugar and heat on medium fire until beef is nicely browned.

Stir in peas and ginger and continue to cook until the liquid is completely absorbed.

To serve, divide rice among individual bowls and top with ground beef mixture.

7. Swedish Meatballs

What makes meatballs in Sweden different from the ones you can find elsewhere? They bathe their meatballs in a creamy and rich sauce packed with comforting and delicious flavors. As a result, the meat melts in the mouth, and you get an insanely satisfying dinner, especially if you pair this dish with rolls, rice, or even pasta.

Serving Size: 6

Prep Time: 30 mins

Ingredients:

- 1 lb. ground beef
- 1 tbsp parsley, finely chopped
- 1/4 cup onion, chopped
- 1/4 cup panko breadcrumbs
- 2 cups beef broth
- 1 cup heavy cream
- 1 tbsp Worcestershire sauce
- 1 tsp Dijon mustard
- 1 pc egg
- 1 tbsp olive oil
- 5 tbsp butter, divided
- 3 tbsp flour
- 1/4 tsp ground nutmeg
- 1/4 tsp ground allspice
- 1/2 tsp garlic powder
- Salt and freshly ground black pepper to taste

Instructions:

Place ground beef, onion, parsley, breadcrumbs, and egg in a bowl. Sprinkle with nutmeg, allspice, garlic powder, and some salt and pepper. Mix until well blended.

Form ground beef mixture into balls and brown in a skillet with olive oil and one tablespoon of butter. Remove meatballs to a plate tented with aluminum foil.

Meanwhile, melt the remaining butter in the same skillet and sprinkle flour. Stir until the flour turns brown.

Gently add beef broth plus cream, Worcestershire sauce, and Dijon mustard, whisking constantly until it comes to a simmer and the sauce starts to become thicker.

Put the meatballs back into the skillet, adjust seasoning to taste, and let it cook for 2-3 minutes or until heated through.

Serve meatballs with sauce over rice or pasta and enjoy.

8. Mongolian Ground Beef

Here is another international recipe made delightful with the use of ground beef. It's a sweet and spicy combo, a favorite takeaway food from different parts of the world. Like the rest, this can be enjoyed with a bowl of steaming hot rice to highlight the best of the dish.

Serving Size: 4

Prep Time: 20 mins

Ingredients:

- 1 lb. lean ground beef
- 2 cups cooked rice
- 1/2 cup scallions, chopped
- 2 tbsp ginger, minced
- 3 garlic cloves, minced
- 1 tsp sesame seeds
- 1 tbsp sesame oil
- 2 tbsp rice vinegar
- 2 tbsp mirin
- 1/4 cup soy sauce
- 1/2 cup brown sugar
- 1/4 tsp red pepper flakes, crushed

Instructions:

Place ground beef in a pan and heat on a medium-high fire.

Remove most of the fat, then stir in ginger and garlic and let it cook for a minute or two.

Pour sesame oil, rice vinegar, mirin, soy sauce, sesame seeds, sugar, and crushed red pepper flakes. Let it cook for a few minutes until most of the liquid has been absorbed.

Toss in scallions and serve over a bowl of hot steamed rice.

9. Chinese Beef Dumplings

Chinese dumplings are favorite takeout food for people who want to eat something nice but do not want to go through the whole nine yards of prepping and cooking. Interestingly, these beef dumplings or potstickers are not as complicated as they may seem. It is definitely manageable and far easier to DIY at home than you think.

Serving Size: 12

Prep Time: 1 hr. 57 mins

Ingredients:

- 1 lb. ground beef
- 50 pcs round dumpling wrappers
- 1/4 cup carrots, shredded
- 1/4 cup frozen peas
- 1/4 cup frozen corn
- 1/2 cup + 1 tbsp green onions, chopped and divided
- 1 tbsp ginger, grated
- 1 tbsp black sesame seeds
- 1 tbsp rice cooking wine
- 1 tsp sesame oil
- 2 tbsp soy sauce
- 2 tbsp vegetable oil
- 1 cup cold water
- 2 tsp sugar
- 1/2 tbsp salt
- 1 tsp white pepper

For the Vinegar Dipping Sauce:

- 1 tbsp green onions, sliced
- 1 tbsp soy sauce
- 2 tbsp black vinegar
- 1 tsp sesame oil

Instructions:

In a large bowl, stir together beef with 1/2 cup of green onions, plus ginger, sesame oil, wine, soy sauce, sugar, salt, and white pepper until well blended.

Stir in carrots, peas, and corn and toss to combine.

Cover the bowl with a sheet of plastic wrap and place in the fridge to chill for at least an hour.

When the meat mixture is ready, take a piece of a dumpling wrapper and place on the flat work surface.

Add about a tablespoon of filling and fold into a half-moon shape, dipping your fingers into some water to keep it moist and make it easier to seal the dumplings in pleats.

Put the dumpling in a parchment paper-lined tray, then repeat with the rest of the wrappers and meat mixture. Get ready with a damp towel to cover the dumplings, so they do not dry out while you take care of the rest.

To cook, heat oil in a nonstick pan (medium-high heat). Add a batch of dumplings in one layer and cook for about three minutes, then flip to the other side until brown and crispy.

Add a splash of water into the pan, cover with a lid, and let it cook for seven minutes until most of the water has evaporated. Repeat the process until all the dumplings are cooked.

To make the dipping sauce, stir together soy sauce, vinegar, sesame oil, and sliced green onions. Stir to blend.

Serve the dumplings with sesame seeds and the remaining green onions on top and the sauce on the side. Enjoy.

10. Beef Shakshuka

Middle Eastern recipes are super interesting. This brunch recipe with eggs, tomatoes, and chilies is great for using ground beef. You can eat this anyway, as is, or with some warm flatbread and fill your tummy with goodness. Interestingly, Shakshuka is a cure for hangovers. That makes it an even better brunch option.

Serving Size: 4

Prep Time: 1 hr. 10 mins

Ingredients:

- 1 lb. ground beef
- 2 cups corn kernels
- 6 pcs ripe tomatoes, diced
- 2 tbsp parsley, flat-leaf, finely chopped
- 2 pcs yellow onion, diced
- 3 garlic cloves, crushed
- 4 pcs chili peppers, chopped
- 1/2 tbsp tomato paste
- 1/2 cup red wine
- 4 pcs eggs
- 1-15oz can red kidney beans
- 2 tbsp olive oil, extra-virgin
- 1 tsp ground cumin
- 1 tbsp paprika
- 1 tsp cayenne pepper
- Coarse salt and freshly ground black pepper to taste

Instructions:

Preheat your oven to 375 degrees F.

Meanwhile, heat oil in an oven-proof skillet over medium fire and sauté onions until soft.

Add ground beef and cook for a few minutes until browned, stirring occasionally.

Sprinkle with paprika, cumin, cayenne, pepper, and salt, and stir.

Add beans and corn, plus chili.

Stir in tomato paste and red wine. Let the pan sizzle, then turn off the fire.

Scatter garlic and tomatoes into the pan and create holes to crack the eggs.

Transfer the skillet onto the preheated oven and let it cook for about five minutes.

While the eggs are still runny, carefully stir to mix everything together.

Put the skillet back into the oven and let it cook until the eggs are set.

Garnish with freshly chopped parsley and serve.

11. Stuffed Cabbage

Ground beef is one of the most delightful ingredients to stuff into things. Cabbage rolls, for example, are made extraordinarily good with ground beef. It is a hearty and tasty dish that you can eat with rice or as is with a side dish of steamed broccoli or mashed potatoes to make your mealtime exciting and complete.

Serving Size: 6

Prep Time: 1 hr. 30 mins

Ingredients:

- 1 lb. ground beef
- 1 head cabbage, leaves separated and blanched
- 1 cup cooked rice
- 1 cup onion, chopped and divided
- 4 garlic cloves, minced and divided
- 1/4 cup fresh parsley, chopped and divided
- 1 pc egg
- 1-28oz can crushed tomatoes
- 1 cup tomato sauce, divided
- 1 tbsp red wine vinegar
- 2 tbsp butter
- Cooking spray
- 2 tbsp brown sugar
- Salt and freshly ground black pepper to taste

Instructions:

To make the sauce, melt butter in a pan over medium fire and sauté half a cup of chopped onions until translucent.

Stir half of the garlic plus crushed tomatoes with all their juices and half a cup of tomato sauce. Season with salt and pepper.

Add sugar and red wine vinegar and stir to blend, then simmer on low heat for 15 minutes with a lid on. Stir occasionally. Set aside.

Meanwhile, combine beef and rice in a large bowl with the remaining onions, garlic, and about two tablespoons of parsley.

Crack the egg into the bowl and add the remaining tomato sauce. Stir until well blended.

Remove the rib of the cabbage leaves and lay a piece on a flat work surface.

Add a few spoonsful of meat mixture and form the cabbage into a log, rolling the leaves and securing the stuffing by putting toothpicks onto the ends. Repeat with the remaining leaves and stuffing.

Preheat your oven to 350 degrees F.

Coat a baking tray with some cooking spray, spoon over half of the prepared tomato sauce at the bottom of the pan, then arrange the stuffed cabbage on top.

Pour the remaining sauce and cover the tray with foil. Bake for an hour and a half, and sprinkle with the remaining parsley before serving.

12. Stuffed Peppers

What's great besides stuffed cabbage? Stuffed Peppers, you bet. This classic recipe is healthy and satisfying. It is ideal for people who are mindful of what they eat, with a savory mix of meat and veggies enhanced by some melted cheese. Even better, you can make this recipe ahead and put it in the freezer, ready to reheat and serve anytime you need to. Let's get down to the recipe!

Serving Size: 6

Prep Time: 1 hr. 5 mins

Ingredients:

- 1 lb. ground beef
- 6 pcs bell peppers
- 2 cups cooked white rice
- 1 and 1/2 cups cheddar cheese, divided
- 1 pc zucchini, diced
- 1/4 cup parsley, finely chopped
- 1/2 cup yellow onion, diced
- 1 tbsp garlic, minced
- 1 tbsp olive oil
- 1 tbsp soy sauce
- 1/2 cup tomato sauce
- Cooking spray
- Salt and freshly ground black pepper to taste

Instructions:

Preheat the oven to 375 degrees F.

To prep the bell peppers, cut the top off, then remove the seeds.

Place the peppers in a baking tray lightly greased with cooking spray and cut the tops up. Set aside.

Meanwhile, heat oil in a pan over medium fire and put in the meat. Brown ground beef, stirring occasionally and breaking apart with the back of the spoon.

Add zucchini, parsley, onion, and garlic. Cook for about two minutes until the veggies are crisp-tender.

Pour in tomato and soy sauces, sprinkle some salt and pepper, and stir to blend.

Simmer the mixture for three minutes, then add rice and half a cup of cheese. Stir to mix evenly. Turn off the fire and let the mixture cool a little.

When the beef mixture is cool enough, start stuffing them onto prepared peppers, cover the top with the remaining cheese, and bake for 40 minutes or until the top is nicely golden.

Let the rest of the stuffed peppers for at least five minutes prior to serving.

13. Beef Rolls

From stuffing ground beef onto veggies to creating a roll completely made up of it. This Beef Rolls recipe may look intimidating at first sight, but it is quite easy to make than you imagine. Serve this with some gravy and you will have a sumptuous dinner to share with everyone in the family. Not one could probably resist the rich meaty taste stuffed into every bite of it.

Serving Size: 6

Prep Time: 55 mins

Ingredients:

- 1 and 1/2 lbs. ground beef
- 2 tbsp onion, finely chopped
- 1/2 cup dry breadcrumbs
- 2 pcs eggs, slightly beaten
- 1 tbsp Worcestershire sauce
- 1/3 cup chicken broth
- 1 cup water
- Cooking spray
- 1-1oz packet brown gravy mix
- 1/4 tsp sage
- 1/4 tsp marjoram
- 1/4 tsp garlic powder
- Salt and freshly ground black pepper to taste

Instructions:

Preheat the oven to 375 degrees F.

In a large mixing bowl, place beef with eggs and Worcestershire sauce. Season with garlic powder, salt, and freshly ground pepper. Mix by the hand until well blended and set aside.

In another bowl, combine onion, breadcrumbs, sage, marjoram, and freshly ground black pepper. Gently add chicken broth and whisk until incorporated.

Divide the meat mixture evenly into six. Working one by one, flatten each portion into a 4-inch square and place it on top of a sheet of wax paper.

Place a suitable amount of the breadcrumb mixture onto each portion and gently roll, keeping the stuffing secure, tucking the seam and the ends. Repeat with the remaining ingredients

Arrange beef rolls in a baking tray lightly greased with some cooking spray. Bake them for 20 minutes or until cooked through.

Meanwhile, gently whisk together gravy mix and water in a saucepan over medium fire. Let it boil until heated through and in a nice consistency.

Transfer beef rolls to a plate, spoon over gravy, and serve.

14. Classic Meatloaf

Another wonderful way to serve ground beef is in a moist, tender-juicy meatloaf. This one is oozing with delicious flavors you could not miss in every crumb. From the meatloaf to the glaze, you will look at ground beef differently if you try making this recipe at home. It will surely become a family favorite.

Serving Size: 8

Prep Time: 1 hr. 30 mins

Ingredients:

- 2 and 1/2 lbs. ground beef
- 1 cup panko breadcrumbs
- 1 pc yellow onion, grated
- 3 cloves garlic, minced
- 1/4 cup parsley, chopped
- 2 pcs eggs
- 1 tsp Worcestershire Sauce
- 3/4 cup tomato ketchup, divided
- 2 tbsp cider vinegar
- 1 tsp dried thyme
- 2 pcs beef bouillon cubes, crumbled
- 1 tbsp brown sugar
- 1 tsp ground black pepper
- Cooking spray

Instructions:

Preheat the oven to 350 degrees F. Prepare a loaf tin lightly greased with cooking spray. Set aside.

In a large bowl, combine beef, breadcrumbs, onions, garlic, eggs, Worcestershire sauce, 1/4 cup of ketchup, parsley, thyme, beef bouillon, and pepper. Mix until well blended.

Form the beef mixture into a loaf and transfer onto the loaf tin, smoothing the creases and cracks to keep it whole.

In a small bowl, whisk together the remaining 1/2 cup of ketchup, plus vinegar and brown sugar, until the sugar is dissolved.

Use half of the glaze mixture to brush the meatloaf generously, then bake for 45 minutes.

Pour the remaining glaze and bake for another 30 minutes. Let it stand at the kitchen counter for at least 10 minutes before slicing and serving.

15. Grilled Beef and Cheese

A grilled cheese sandwich is delightful. But add a stuffing of some ground beef into your sandwich, and you will take it to a whole new different level. Suddenly, it is not a simple sandwich anymore. It becomes a delightful treat you can serve to make game nights interesting or have with friends over to share a tasty snack.

Serving Size: 4

Prep Time: 30 mins

Ingredients:

- 1 lb. ground beef
- 8 pcs white bread slices
- 8 pcs Swiss cheese slices
- 1 cup button mushrooms, chopped
- 1/2 pc onion, finely chopped
- 1 garlic clove, minced
- 4 tsp butter, divided

Instructions:

Place beef and mushrooms, plus onion and garlic, in a nonstick pan and heat on medium fire.

Stir to brown for about five minutes.

Remove beef mixture to a plate using a slotted spoon and set aside. Discard the fat in the pan and wipe it clean.

Add about a teaspoon of butter into the pan and let it melt on medium fire. Add two slices of bread, then flip.

Place a slice of cheese on one bread, top with about 1/3 cup of the beef mixture, and cover with the other piece of bread to make a sandwich. Cook until the cheese melts nicely, then repeat with the remaining bread, cheese, and ground beef filling.

Serve and enjoy.

16. Meatball Sub Sandwich

What's better than eating meatballs? Eating meatballs in a sandwich. Now, here's the deal: You make meatballs from ground beef and other ingredients, cook them in marinara sauce and then stuff them into hoagie rolls. Do you get the picture? For sure, we got your craving so let's make the recipe.

Serving Size: 6

Prep Time: 35 mins

Ingredients:

- 1 lb. ground beef
- 1/2 lb. Italian sausage, casings removed and crumbled
- 6 pc hoagie rolls
- 4 cloves garlic, minced
- 1/3 cup Italian parsley, finely chopped
- 1/2 cup breadcrumbs
- 3/4 cup Parmesan cheese, grated
- 8 oz mozzarella cheese, shredded
- 3 cups marinara sauce
- 1 pc egg
- 4 tbsp olive oil
- 2 tsp garlic powder
- 1 tsp salt
- 1 tsp freshly ground pepper

Instructions:

In a large mixing bowl, place beef, sausage, breadcrumbs, Parmesan, parsley, garlic, egg, salt, and pepper. Stir until well blended.

Form mixture into balls, then place in a saucepan and pour in marinara sauce.

Cover with a lid and cook in a simmer on medium fire for ten minutes. Take off the lid and let the meatballs cook for ten minutes more.

Brush the inside of hoagie rolls with some olive oil. Sprinkle with a bit of garlic powder. Arrange rolls in a baking tray, and top with 4-6 meatballs and some mozzarella.

Preheat the broiler and place the baking tray into the broiler to melt the cheese.

Serve hot and enjoy.

17. Juicy Hamburger

This ground beef cookbook will be lacking without a hamburger recipe. But this is not just your ordinary recipe. We picked the best to give you something to look forward to during snack time. Serve this to your family and give them something delicious to feast on.

Serving Size: 6

Prep Time: 25 mins

Ingredients:

- 1 and 1/2 lbs. ground beef
- 6 pcs hamburger buns, split in half and lightly toasted
- 6 pcs cheddar cheese slices
- 6 pcs lettuce leaves
- 6 pcs pickle slices
- 1 pc beefsteak tomato, sliced
- 1/2 pc white onion, thinly sliced
- 2 tsp paprika
- 1/4 tsp onion powder
- 1/4 tsp garlic powder
- 1/4 tsp cayenne pepper
- 1/2 tsp brown sugar
- 1 tsp salt
- 1 and 1/2 tsp freshly ground black pepper

Instructions:

In a small bowl, combine paprika, onion powder, garlic powder, cayenne pepper, brown sugar, salt, and pepper.

Divide ground beef into six portions and form into hamburger patties. Make sure the patties are slightly bigger than the buns because they will shrink during the cooking process.

Preheat the grill to high. Before placing the burger patties on the hot grill, sprinkle both sides with the prepared seasoning.

Grill the patties for about 8 minutes total, flipping to the other side halfway. Cover with the lid.

Before the patties are cooked through, place a cheese slice on each and let it melt a little. Rest the patties before making the burgers.

To assemble, place the lettuce leaves at the bottom of the buns, and top with burger patties, pickles, tomatoes, and onions.

Serve and enjoy.

18. Lasagna Soup

Ground beef is perfect for burgers and sandwiches, but they also make a nice ingredient in soups. This Lasagna Soup is a great example of a warm and comforting dish that will melt your family's heart. It's a delicious substitute for the usual lasagna. Try it to believe it!

Serving Size: 8

Prep Time: 40 mins

Ingredients:

- 1/2 lb. lean ground beef
- 1 lb. Italian sausage, casings removed
- 8 pcs lasagna noodles, cooked according to package directions
- 8 oz mozzarella, shredded
- 1/3 cup Parmesan cheese
- 1 tbsp fresh parsley, optional
- 1 pc onion, diced
- 6 garlic cloves, minced
- 1-28oz can crushed tomatoes
- 1-14oz can tomato sauce
- 1-6oz can tomato paste
- 4 cups chicken broth
- 1 tbsp olive oil
- 2 tsp Italian seasoning
- 1 tsp fennel seeds
- 2 tsp salt
- 12 tsp ground black pepper

Instructions:

Heat oil in a stockpot over medium fire.

Add ground beef and sausage, plus onions, and cook for about eight minutes or until nicely browned, stirring occasionally and crumbling the meat with the back of the spoon.

Stir in garlic and cook for another minute or two.

Pour canned tomatoes with their juices, tomato sauce, tomato paste, and chicken broth. Then, season with Italian seasoning, fennel, salt, and pepper.

Turn up the heat and let the mixture boil, then simmer on low for 20 minutes, covered with a lid.

Add lasagna noodles, mozzarella, and Parmesan cheeses into the pot, stir, and simmer for a few more minutes.

Ladle soup into bowls, garnish with freshly chopped parsley and serve.

19. Taco Soup

Another delicious ground beef soup is made with the flavors of Mexican tacos. It is another comforting and hearty meal you can serve to warm up your dinner and make it more inviting. You can do this with the usual taco toppings, or you may add other ingredients as you like to suit your palate. And this dish even comes with a bonus: it is so easy to make!

Serving Size: 6

Prep Time: 35 mins

Ingredients:

- 1 lb. ground beef
- 1-28oz can black beans, rinsed and drained
- 1 cup corn kernels
- 1 pc avocado, thinly sliced
- 1 cup tortilla chips
- 1/4 cup cheddar cheese, shredded
- 1/4 cup fresh cilantro, chopped
- 1 pc onion, diced
- 1 tbsp garlic, minced
- 1 pc jalapeño pepper, finely diced
- 1 pc lime, sliced into wedges
- 2 -14oz cans crushed tomatoes
- 3 tbsp Greek yogurt
- 1 and 3/4 cups beef broth
- 2 tbsp olive oil
- 1 tsp ground cumin
- 1 tsp paprika
- 1 tsp red pepper flakes, crushed
- 1 tsp salt
- 1/2 tsp freshly ground black pepper

Instructions:

Heat olive oil in a stock pot over medium fire and brown ground beef for about seven minutes. Crumble the meat using the back of the spoon to brown them evenly.

Stir in onion, garlic, and jalapeño and cook for another two minutes.

Season mixture with cumin, paprika, crushed red pepper flakes, salt, and pepper. Stir and cook for another minute.

Gently pour broth and crushed tomatoes with all their juices. Boil, turn heat to low, and simmer for 10 minutes with the lid on.

Stir in corn and black beans and simmer for five minutes more.

Ladle taco soup into individual bowls, and top with avocado slices, tortilla chips, cilantro, and cheese. Dot soup with yogurt and serve with lime wedges on the side.

20. Hamburger Stroganoff

If you think a hamburger is great enough, turn them into a stroganoff dish. You will be amazed by the different appeal of these yummy burgers bathing in a luscious sauce. You can eat this dish with rice, pasta, or rolls and let your family enjoy a hearty dinner they deserve after an exhausting day at school or work.

Serving Size: 4

Prep Time: 1 hr. 5 mins

Ingredients:

- 1 lb. ground beef
- 2 cups dried penne pasta, cooked according to package directions
- 1 pc carrot, diced
- 10oz white mushrooms, quartered
- 1 pc onion, chopped
- 3 garlic cloves, finely chopped
- 3 tbsp fresh parsley, chopped
- 3 tbsp fresh chives, chopped
- 1-15oz can beef broth
- 1 tbsp tomato paste
- 1 tbsp Worcestershire sauce
- 2oz cream cheese, at room temperature
- 1/4 cup sour cream
- 1 tbsp extra-virgin olive oil
- 1 and 1/2 cups water
- 1/2 tsp paprika
- Kosher salt and freshly ground black pepper to taste

Instructions:

Place ground beef in a nonstick skillet with paprika, plus some salt and pepper and heat on medium. Cook until browned, stirring occasionally. Remove to a plate using a slotted spoon and set aside.

Add oil to the beef drippings and sauté mushrooms in the same pan. Sprinkle with salt and cook for eight minutes, stirring occasionally.

Add carrot, onion, and garlic and cook for another ten minutes.

Pour in tomato paste and stir for another two minutes.

Gently pour in the broth, plus Worcestershire sauce and water. Put back the beef and simmer on low for ten minutes, covered with a lid.

Add cooked pasta, plus cream cheese, and sour cream.

Stir in parsley and chives, adjust seasoning, then turn off the fire.

Serve and enjoy.

21. Shepherd's Pie

From international recipes to stuffing, sandwiches, and soups, we are now giving you some classic recipes that cry for ground beef to keep you even more excited, starting with Shepherd's Pie. This delicious recipe made of beef, veggies, mashed potatoes, and gravy can be a handful to make, but it is worth the effort. And don't worry because it will not take too long to make. All you need is a little over an hour, and that's it.

Serving Size: 6

Prep Time: 1 hr. 10 mins

Ingredients:

Meat Filling:

- 2 tbsp olive oil
- 1 cup yellow onion, chopped
- 1 lb. lean ground beef
- 2 lbs. russet potatoes, peeled and cubed
- 1 cup frozen peas and carrots, thawed
- 1/2 cup corn kernels
- 2 cloves garlic, minced
- 1/4 cup Parmesan cheese, grated
- 8 tbsp unsalted butter
- 2 tbsp tomato paste
- 1 tbsp Worcestershire sauce
- 1 cup beef broth
- 1/3 cup half & half
- 2 tsp dried parsley leaves
- 1 tsp dried rosemary leaves
- 1 tsp dried thyme leaves
- 1/2 tsp garlic powder
- Salt and freshly ground black pepper to taste

Instructions:

Heat oil in a nonstick skillet on medium-high and sauté onions for two minutes. Add beef and cook until browned, about five minutes, stirring occasionally.

Sprinkle rosemary, parsley, thyme, and some salt and pepper to taste. Cook for eight minutes.

Add garlic and Worcestershire sauce and cook for a minute more.

Add corn kernels, peas and carrots, tomato paste, and broth. Boil, then reduce to a simmer for ten minutes or until the meat is tender.

Meanwhile, boil potatoes in a pot of lightly salted water until tender.

Transfer potatoes to a bowl and add Parmesan, butter, half & half, plus garlic powder. Season with salt and pepper. Mash until the ingredients are well blended.

To assemble, transfer the meat mixture into an oven-proof casserole and spread out in an even layer.

Spoon mashed potatoes and spread evenly.

Preheat the oven to 375 degrees F.

Bake the pie for about half an hour, let it cool for 15 minutes, and serve.

22. Ground Beef and Broccoli Stir-Fry

Another classic recipe worth including in this ground beef cookbook is this one with broccoli. It may be a simple stir-fry recipe, but if done right, it could make an impression at the dinner table. This is best prepared during those busy weeknights when you need to make dinner but are too tired to do something elaborate.

Serving Size: 4

Prep Time: 20 mins

Ingredients:

- 1 lb. ground beef
- 12oz broccoli florets, chopped into small pieces
- 2 cups cooked rice
- 2 pcs green onions, chopped
- 1 tsp sesame seeds
- 4 cloves garlic, minced
- 1/4 cup soy sauce
- 2 tsp sesame oil
- 2 tsp corn starch
- 1 tsp ground ginger
- 1/4 tsp red pepper flakes, crushed
- 1 tbsp brown sugar

Instructions:

Place ground beef in a nonstick skillet and heat on medium-high, breaking into pieces using the back of the spoon. Discard the grease and put the beef back into the skillet. Let it cook on medium-low fire for a few more minutes.

Meanwhile, in a small bowl, combine soy sauce, sesame oil, ginger, garlic, corn starch, brown sugar, and crushed red pepper flakes and stir until the sugar is dissolved.

Turn up the heat to high and pour prepared sauce plus the broccoli florets. Let it sizzle and cook for a few minutes until broccoli is crisp-tender.

To serve, divide rice among individual bowls, spoon over beef broccoli, and garnish with green onions and sesame seeds.

23. Creamy Ground Beef and Shells

Pasta and ground beef have a long history together. You cannot make delicious spaghetti without ground beef. But more than just your usual spaghetti, or spaghetti with meatballs, which others prefer, you can mix pasta and ground beef and get a different result. This creamy pasta dish is one for the books. It's a delicious recipe that both kids and adults would love earnestly.

Serving Size: 4

Prep Time: 40 mins

Ingredients:

- 8oz pasta shells, cooked according to package directions
- 1 tbsp olive oil
- 1 lb. ground beef
- 1/2 pc sweet onion, diced
- 2 garlic cloves, minced
- 1 and 1/2 cups extra-sharp cheddar cheese, shredded
- 3/4 cup heavy cream
- 1-15oz can tomato sauce
- 2 cups beef stock
- 2 tbsp all-purpose flour
- 1 and 1/2 tsp Italian seasoning
- Kosher salt and black pepper to taste

Instructions:

Heat oil in a nonstick skillet over a medium-high fire and brown ground beef for five minutes.

Stir in onions and cook until soft and translucent for three minutes.

Add garlic and sprinkle Italian seasoning; cook for a minute or two.

Sprinkle flour and stir for another minute.

Gradually pour the stock, whisking gently, then add tomato sauce.

Boil the mixture, then turn the heat to low and simmer for eight minutes or until the sauce thickens.

Add cooked pasta, cheese, and heavy cream into the skillet and let it cook until heated through. Season with salt and pepper.

Serve and enjoy.

24. Ground Beef Pasta Skillet

If you are looking for a quick and easy pasta dish that's easy on the budget, this is the perfect recipe for you. It has pasta, beef, and veggies—a complete meal in one that prepares in about 30 minutes. Cooking this pasta dish is one of the simplest ways to impress your family at the dinner table. Let's start!

Serving Size: 6

Prep Time: 30 mins

Ingredients:

- 1 lb. ground beef
- 1-14oz package mac and cheese, cooked according to package directions
- 2 cups corn kernels
- 1 pc green bell pepper, seeded and diced
- 1 pc onion, finely diced
- 1 garlic clove, minced or grated
- 1-14.5oz can diced tomatoes, drained
- 1-15oz can tomato sauce

Instructions:

Place beef, bell pepper, onion, and garlic in a nonstick skillet and heat on medium-high, stirring often until the beef is browned.

Add corn, tomatoes, and tomato sauce and stir. Let the mixture simmer for five minutes.

Stir in cooked macaroni and cheese and mix to blend.

Serve while hot.

25. Classic Spaghetti

This ground beef recipe book will never be complete without the Classic Spaghetti. This one is exactly the dish you remember eating as a kid. It is your favorite comfort food, which you can use to impress your family this time around.

Serving Size: 8

Prep Time: 1 hr. 30 mins

Ingredients:

- 1 and 1/2 lbs. ground beef
- 16oz spaghetti, cooked according to package directions
- 1/2 cup Parmesan cheese, grated
- 2 tbsp parsley, finely chopped
- 1 pc green bell pepper, seeded and finely chopped
- 1 and 1/2 cups onion, chopped
- 1 tbsp garlic, minced
- 1-28oz can crushed tomatoes
- 1-6oz can tomato paste
- 1-16oz can tomato sauce
- 1 tbsp Italian seasoning
- 1/2 tsp granulated sugar
- 1 and 1/2 tsp salt
- 1/2 tsp black pepper

Instructions:

Place beef in a nonstick skillet and heat on medium-high until nicely browned.

Sprinkle with salt and pepper and stir for a few minutes more. Remove beef and transfer to a plate using a slotted spoon.

Remove much of the grease, leaving only about two tablespoons for sautéing, then add bell peppers, onion, and garlic, and cook for about five minutes or until the onion is soft and translucent.

Put back the beef into the pan and add crushed tomatoes with their juices, plus tomato paste and tomato sauce. Sprinkle with Italian seasoning and sugar and stir. Let it boil for a minute, then turn the heat to low and simmer for about an hour. Add more salt and pepper as preferred.

Toss cooked spaghetti into the sauce, top with Parmesan and some freshly chopped parsley, and serve.

26. Beef Lasagna

Lasagna is another classic dish made wonderful with ground beef. But unlike the common impression, it is not as difficult to make. Many cooks get overwhelmed with the processes involved in preparing the dish. That's why we chose this recipe to convince you that making lasagna at home will not tire you so much that you will no longer be able to enjoy it.

Serving Size: 12

Prep Time: 1 hr. 20 mins

Ingredients:

- 1 lb. ground beef
- 1 pc onion, diced
- 2 tbsp dried oregano, divided
- 1/2 tsp salt
- 1/2 tsp ground pepper
- 1-24oz marinara sauce
- 1 cup water
- 15oz ricotta cheese
- 2 pcs eggs
- 1/2 cup Parmesan cheese, grated
- 12 pcs lasagna noodles
- 2 cups mozzarella cheese, shredded

Instructions:

Preheat the oven to 375 degrees F.

Place ground beef in a nonstick skillet and heat on medium fire. Stir to brown for about eight minutes.

Add onion, one tablespoon of dried oregano, plus salt and pepper. Cook for another three to five minutes or until the onion is soft and translucent.

Pour in marinara sauce and water. Stir and let it boil. Turn off the fire and set it aside.

Meanwhile, stir together the remaining dried oregano, ricotta cheese, eggs, and Parmesan. Season with some salt and pepper and mix until well blended.

Assemble the lasagna by starting with a ladle of marinara sauce, spreading evenly. Top with three pieces of noodles, then the ricotta mixture and 1/2 cup of shredded mozzarella. Repeat the layer until all the ingredients are used, ending up with cheese.

Bake for about an hour, let it rest a couple of minutes, and serve.

27. Ground Beef Nachos

If you want to enjoy ground beef as a snack, you can do with more than just burgers and sandwiches. Nachos, a Mexican classic, are a favorite snack, best made with ground beef. In this recipe, we are making a nice layer of tortillas, meat, veggies, cheese, and sauce, giving you different textures and tastes that are loveable and alluring to the palate.

Serving Size: 4

Prep Time: 25 mins

Ingredients:

- 1/2 lb. ground beef
- 1 tbsp olive oil
- 1-12oz bag tortilla chips
- 1 pc avocado, peeled, stoned, and diced
- 1/2 cup tomato, diced
- 2 tbsp green onion, chopped
- 2 tbsp pickled jalapeños, chopped
- 1 and 1/2 cups Mexican cheese blend
- 1/2 cup sour cream
- 1/2 tsp ground cumin
- 1/4 tsp garlic powder
- 1/2 tsp chili powder
- Pinch of cayenne pepper
- 1 tsp kosher salt
- 1/2 tsp black pepper

Instructions:

Preheat the oven to 400 degrees F.

Meanwhile, heat oil in a skillet over medium-high and brown ground beef. Stir occasionally and break apart meat using the back of the spoon to brown evenly.

Sprinkle with cumin, garlic powder, chili powder, cayenne, salt, and pepper. Mix to blend.

To assemble, arrange tortilla chips in a baking tray and top with ground beef and cheese.

Bake for about ten minutes until the cheese is melty.

Scatter nachos with avocadoes, tomatoes, jalapeños, and green onions.

Dot with sour cream and serve.

28. Ground Beef and Cabbage Salad

Here is an Asian-inspired salad to keep your meal plans completely. It is a delicious mix of napa cabbage and ground beef, bathed in plum sauce. This is a fantastic option to turn to if you want to serve something different, a notch higher than your usual salad dishes. It's delicious, crunchy, quick, and easy to make.

Serving Size: 4

Prep Time: 25 mins

Ingredients:

- 1 lb. ground beef
- 8 cups Napa cabbage, shredded
- 2 pcs carrots, thinly sliced
- 4 pcs scallions, sliced
- 1 cup cilantro, chopped
- 1/4 cup plum sauce
- 1/2 cup rice vinegar
- 1/4 cup canola oil
- Salt and freshly ground black pepper to taste

Instructions:

Brown ground beef in a skillet on medium-high and pour plum sauce. Set aside.

In a small bowl, whisk together vinegar and oil. Season with salt and pepper. Set aside.

In a salad bowl, stir together cabbage, carrots, scallions, and cilantro.

Pour vinegar-oil mixture and toss.

Scatter ground beef on top and serve.

29. Spicy Ground Beef & Cucumber Salad

Another salad dish with ground beef is this cucumber salad, which is quite popular because it can be served as a main dish rather than a side. It has high protein and low carbohydrate content, making it the perfect meal option for people on a diet.

Serving Size: 2

Prep Time: 35 mins

Ingredients:

- 2 tbsp coconut oil
- 1/2 pc brown onion, finely diced
- 1/2 pc long red chill, finely diced
- 1 lb. ground beef
- 4 pcs cucumber, diced
- 1/2 cup raw cashews
- 2 tbsp cilantro, diced
- 10 pcs fresh mint leaves
- 3 garlic cloves, finely diced
- 1 tsp tomato paste
- 2 tbsp olive oil
- 1 tbsp lemon juice
- 1/2 tsp paprika
- 1 tsp ground coriander seeds
- 1 tsp ground cumin
- Pinch of ground cinnamon
- Pinch of ground cloves
- 1 tsp sea salt
- 1/2 tsp ground black pepper

For the cashew dressing:

- 3/4 cup raw cashews, soaked in hot water for an hour
- 1 clove garlic, diced
- 3/4 tsp tahini paste
- Juice of 1 pc lemon
- 2 tbsp water
- Pinch of sea salt

Instructions:

To make the cashew dressing, place all the ingredients in a blender or food processor and pulse until smooth. Add a splash more water if needed to attain the desired consistency. Set aside.

Meanwhile, heat coconut oil in a skillet over medium-high and sauté onion and chili for five minutes.

Stir in ground beef, breaking apart with the back of the spoon, and garlic. Let it cook for another five minutes until the meat is evenly browned.

Add tomato paste, then sprinkle with paprika, cumin, coriander seeds, cinnamon, cloves, salt, and pepper. Stir to blend. Set aside to cool down.

To assemble the salad, combine cucumber, cashew, and cilantro in a serving tray. Drizzle with lemon juice and olive and toss to combine.

Scatter beef on cucumber mix and toss gently.

Add a few dollops of cashew dressing and a garnish of mint before serving.

30. Lettuce Wraps

This dish is for you if you want something creative, whether to serve to guests or just to make your mealtime more interesting. It's a presentable salad to make the buffet table look nice. And like much of the recipes in this cookbook, it does not take up much time to prepare. All you need is 20 minutes, and you are ready to serve.

Serving Size: 4

Prep Time: 20 mins

Ingredients:

- 1 and 1/2 lbs. lean ground beef
- 1 head butter lettuce, leaves separated
- 1 cup mushrooms, minced
- 1 pc red bell pepper, seeded and diced
- 1-8oz can water chestnuts, diced
- 1/2 cup cashews, chopped
- 2 pcs green onions, chopped
- 2 cloves garlic, minced
- 1 tbsp sesame oil
- 1/4 cup soy sauce
- 1 tbsp rice vinegar
- 1/8 tsp garlic chili paste
- 1/4 tsp ground ginger

Instructions:

Heat oil in a skillet over medium fire and sauté onions, mushroom, and red bell pepper. Let it cook for five minutes until cooked through.

Stir in ground beef and cook until evenly browned, breaking apart the meat with the back of the spoon.

Add chestnuts and garlic and cook for another two minutes.

Pour in the vinegar, soy sauce, garlic-chili paste, and ground ginger. Cook for about four minutes, stirring occasionally.

To serve, arrange lettuce leaves in a serving tray, spoon over ground beef mixture, and garnish with cashew nuts and green onions.

Conclusion

Ground beef is a perennial favorite among the many available types of meat and meat cuts. Why not? This is pretty easy to handle. You can make it into many different dishes for various courses, and they are all extremely mouthwatering. It is also inexpensive compared to other cuts.

Cooking ground beef takes only a few minutes. After a few minutes of browning properly, the meat is good, as in tender-juicy good. Then, you will just have to take care of the rest of the steps, and your recipes are done, usually in less than an hour. Only recipes with complicated processes will make your stay in the kitchen for an hour or more. But that's comparably still a short time.

There are also lots of ground beef recipes to choose from. This cookbook only contains 30, but you have countless more choices available, from salad to snacks to breakfast, lunch, dinner, and more. Cooking with ground beef is one of the most amazing options you can find to prepare delicious quick, and easy meals during busy weeknights.

Best of all, ground beef does not cost that much. You can get them for a portion of the sum you usually pay to get other beef cuts and meat varieties. That's why it's the go-to ingredient not just for people who have limited time but also a limited budget.

If you are still not convinced that cooking with ground beef is a great grind, try at least one of the recipes in this cookbook. You will know what we are talking about if you do.

Happy cooking!

Epilogues

There are days I feel like quitting, but then I remember readers like you, and my heart swells with pride at the love you show me by buying each and every book I put out there.

I am delighted, to say the least, to know that people like you take their time to download, read and cook with my books!

Thank you so much for accepting me and all that I have shared with the world.

While I am basking in the euphoria of your love and commitment to my books, I would beseech you to kindly drop your reviews and feedback. I would love to read from you!

Head to Amazon.com to drop your reviews!!!

Thank you

Charlotte Long

About the Author

For the past 10 years, Charlotte has been collating and exploring different dishes from different cultures of the world. Birthed and raised in Ohio, Charlotte grew up to know that cooking is a magical activity that requires a certain degree of commitment and love to be carried out.

She learnt this from her grandmother who was one of the best local chefs in Ohio then. Charlotte's grandmother would always create and invent new recipes and also refurbish old ones. The result of it is her passion for cooking cum a large book of special recipes that Charlotte inherited.

Using her grandmother's recipe book as her foundational training guide, Charlotte wore her grandmother's chef shoes to become one of the best chefs in Ohio and its environment.

Charlotte has written different recipe books, and she is currently touring the Caribbean and looking for new recipes to unravel.

Printed in Great Britain
by Amazon